# Bach

## Prelude in C Major

*from* The Well-Tempered Clavier

Cover photography: Copyright © 1998 Matt Harris/Panoramic Images, Chicago
All Rights Reserved.

Project editor: Peter Pickow

Copyright © 1999 by Amsco Publications,
A Division of Music Sales Corporation, New York

Order No. AM 948630
International Standard Book Number: 978.0.8256.1731.7

**Music Sales America**

DISTRIBUTED BY

**HAL•LEONARD®**
CORPORATION

7777 W. BLUEMOUND RD. P.O. BOX 13819 MILWAUKEE, WI 53213

# Prelude in C Major

*from* The Well-Tempered Clavier

J.S. Bach